The Adventures of Winston, the Little Black Poodle

Winston Runs Away

CELESTE M. GROS

Illustrations by Gennel Marie Sollano

Illustrated by Gennel Marie Sollano

To order additional copies of this book, contact:
Xlibris
844-714-8691
www.Xlibris.com
Orders@Xlibris.com

ISBN: Softcover   978-1-6641-5273-1
            Hardcover   978-1-6641-5275-5
            EBook   978-1-6641-5274-8

Print information available on the last page

Rev. date: 01/21/2021

The Adventures of Winston, the Little Black Poodle

Winston Runs Away

CELESTE M. GROS

Hi everyone! I'm Winston and I'm a little black Poodle! Being curious is what I do best and it's gotten me into some really crazy moments. Today I will share with you one of my very first adventures!

I was new to my family and was getting very spoiled. My Mommy wanted to take a trip with my Daddy and decided to leave me with the groomer for a few days. Now I love my groomer, Ms. Keri, but I love my Mommy more and didn't want to be away from her.

Mommy dropped me off late one afternoon and I was really sad and lonely. I missed her so much. When Ms. Keri was busy, I decided to try and get back home to my Mommy but little did I know it wasn't going to be that easy.

I quickly realized I could slip through the bars of the gate and once on the other side, I took off running!

I ran and ran but didn't know exactly where I was going. I knew we lived by a river, but so did Ms. Keri. After a while, I got really confused and scared and didn't know what to do.

As I ran, cars were whisking by me really fast and there were other dogs barking and growling at me. Every so often I would slip behind a tree or under a house, but I never stopped running. Keeping the water in my sight was what I needed to do to find my home, but as I ran, the sky got darker and darker. It was getting very late and soon it would be nighttime. I kept thinking to myself, "I want my Mommy so bad!"

Running was getting me really tired,
so I found a big box on the side of
the road and slipped in it and drifted
off to sleep.

8

All of a sudden, there was a loud noise that woke me up. The box started to bounce around and I didn't know what to do.

Once it stopped, I peeked out of the box and there was the biggest cat I had ever seen in my life. I'm so little that almost anything is big to me.

The big cat was jumping on top the box, then off the box, then back on top, just bouncing me all around! He knew something was in that box and wanted to find out what it was and that something was me!

11

As I crawled out of the box the big cat hissed at me first then said "Hey little puppy. What are you doing out along at night? You're too little to be away from your home." With a scared and nervous voice, I said "My Mommy left me at a friend's house and I missed her so bad and wanted to go home, so I ran away." "That wasn't very smart of you, little puppy." the cat quickly replied.

I lowered my head because I knew the big cat was right. I made a big mistake by leaving Ms. Keri's house and I knew she would be very worried and when my Mommy finds out she would be worried too.

After we chatted for a little while, I decided to take off again on my journey to get home. I started running real fast and finally got to a big bridge.

14

I stopped and took a good look at it and thought, "How am I going to cross this bridge?" As I slowly crept closer to it, I realized the sides of the bridge were solid and that way my little feet wouldn't slip through any of the cracks like there were on the middle part of the bridge.

15

It was still nighttime so no one would see me crossing it so off I went, running with all my might to cross this big bridge.

Once on the other side, I knew I had to stay close to the water and that way I would get home.

Little did I know at that time, the river I was running along wasn't the same river that was by my house, but the need to get home and see my Mommy was too great to stop me from trying. As I ran, I search for anything familiar that would tell me I was home but as the sun began to rise, I knew something was terribly wrong.

Nothing I saw, looked like home. I was tired, hungry, scared and dirty from running through mud and water. My little paws were hurting and I was feeling like I would never get to see my Mommy again.

Up ahead I saw what looked like a pier, just like the one we had at home, so I took off running faster trying to get to it.

When I reached the pier, I stopped running and sat down breathing heavily and started to cry. I realized this wasn't our pier. I didn't know if I would ever find it. I kept thinking to myself, "Where is my Mommy? I miss her so very much and if I ever get to go home, I will never run away again!"

Sitting there crying, I never saw the lady that was walking towards me. I stood up and started to back away from her, but if I backed up too much I would fall in the river so I stopped and put my head down.

She slowly walked closer with her hand extended out and started to talk to me very slowly and very sweetly. I was so scared, tired and hungry and she seemed so nice that if I was going to get home, I just needed to trust her.

"Maybe she knows my Mommy." I kept thinking. "Maybe she could take me home." I had to get home and this may be the only way for me to see my Mommy and Daddy again.

"Hey Winston." She said very sweetly. "How does she know my name?" I thought. "Come here little fellow. There are a lot of people looking for you." Slowly I eased up to her. She never moved any closer but let me walk closer to her. Once I was within her reach, I felt her hands around me, slowly picking me up. The lady was indeed very sweet and gentle.

She then took me to her office where she gave me a bowl of water and a little something to nibble on until my groomer, Ms. Keri, could come by and pick me up.

I was a very lucky little black poodle that day. There are so many things that could have happened to me but God was looking out for this little boy! I finally was reunited with my Mommy and Daddy and as my Mommy cried with joy, I really felt bad that I had hurt her and everyone else. From that day on I made a promise to myself to never do anything like this again.

So my friends, take it from me. Listen to your Mommy and Daddy and never try to run away from them or anyone they leave you with. There are a lot of things that could happen to you. I learned a big lesson during my journey to get home and was very thankful that I could get home safely.

Now I am a very happy little black Poodle, staying close to my Mommy and Daddy.

Printed in the United States
By Bookmasters